Will the Sun Ever Burn Out?

Earth, Sun, and Moon

Rosalind Mist

www.heinemann.co.uk/library
Visit our website to find out more information about Heinemann Library books.

To order:
☎ Phone 44 (0) 1865 888066
▤ Send a fax to 44 (0) 1865 314091
▢ Visit the Heinemann Bookshop at www.heinemann.co.uk/library to browse our catalogue and order online.

First published in Great Britain by Heinemann Library, Halley Court, Jordan Hill, Oxford OX2 8EJ, part of Harcourt Education. Heinemann is a registered trademark of Harcourt Education Ltd.

Editorial: Nancy Dickmann and Sarah Chappelow
Design: Richard Parker and Tinstar Design
Illustrations: Jeff Edwards
Picture Research: Erica Newbery and Kay Altwegg
Production: Camilla Crask

Originated by Chroma Graphics (Overseas) Pte Ltd.
Printed in China by WKT Company Limited

10 digit ISBN: 0 431 18186 1
13 digit ISBN: 978 0 431 18186 8

10 09 08 07 06
10 9 8 7 6 5 4 3 2 1

British Library Cataloguing in Publication Data
Rosalind Mist
Will the sun ever burn out?
– (Stargazer Guides)
523.7
A full catalogue record for this book is available from the British Library.

Acknowledgements
The publishers would like to thank the following for permission to reproduce photographs: Corbis pp. **22** (John Carnemolla/Australian Picture Library), **32** (Rob Howard), **34**, **36** (Bob Krist); Galaxy pp. **8**(D. Roddy/Lpi), **11** (NASA), **13** (Johnson Space Centre), **14** (Kipp Teague/David Woods/NASA), **15** (NASA), **18** (Soho/NASA/Esa), **35** (Robin Scagell), **42** (Andrea Dupree/ Ronald Gilliland (Stsci)/ NASA/Esa); Getty Images/Photodisc pp, **4**, **6**, **28** (Arnulf Husmo), **29**, **33**, **38**; Harcourt Index p. **7**; Scala p. **31**; Science Photo Library pp. **5**, **7** (Roger Harris), **9** (Pekka Parviainen), **10** (David Nunuk), **12** (Mark Garlick), **16** (Eckhard Slawik), **19** (Mehau Kulyk), **20** (National Optical Astronomy Observatories), **21** (NASA), **23** (Detlev Van Ravenswaay), **24**, **25** (Royal Swedish Academy Of Sciences), **26** (Detlev Van Ravenswaay), **27** (NASA), **39** (Detlev Van Ravenswaay), **40** (John Chumack), **41** (Mark Garlick), **43** (Joe Tucciarone), **44** (John Sanford).

Cover image of the Sun reproduced with permission of the Science Photo Library.

The publishers would like to thank Dr. Geza Gyuk of the Adler Planetarium in Chicago for his assistance in the preparation of this book.

The paper used to print this book comes from sustainable resources.

Contents

Words appearing in the text in bold, **like this**, are explained in the Glossary.

Looking up at the sky

If it is clear outside, go out and look up at the sky. What can you see? From Earth, the brightest and biggest things in the sky are the Sun and the Moon. The Sun and Moon are giant spheres (balls) moving through space. The Earth is a giant ball, too. But these three balls are very different sizes and are made of different things.

The Sun is the biggest ball of the three. It is a star – a huge burning ball of gas. The Earth is next in size. It is over 100 times smaller than the Sun. It is a **planet**. It is made of rock rather than gas, with oceans covering much of the surface. A thin layer of air (the **atmosphere**) surrounds the Earth. The smallest ball is the Moon. It is about a quarter the size of the Earth. The Moon is solid rock, but it has no oceans or atmosphere.

The Sun's surface is not smooth. Coils of hot, fiery material reach out into space.

Seen from afar, the Moon is a land of rocks and craters, while the Earth has clouds swirling above green land and blue sea.

Our home

The Earth is our home. It is the only place in the Universe where we know there is life. But without the Sun, this life would not exist. The Sun pours out huge amounts of light and heat energy. Some of this energy warms the Earth and gives us light. Without heat and light, life could not survive here.

The Moon does not give us any energy, but through the ages people have used it to help keep track of time.

Gravity, keeping things together

The Sun is the centre of our **Solar System**. The Earth and other planets all **orbit** (go round) the Sun. The Moon orbits the Earth.

The **force** that keeps the Solar System together is **gravity**. Gravity is a pulling force that acts between any two objects. The more massive (heavy) something is, the stronger the pull of its gravity. The Sun is so massive that it can keep all the planets, **moons**, and **asteroids** orbiting around it. The Earth has enough **mass** to keep the Moon in orbit around it.

The Earth

The Earth is about 4.5 billion years old. It formed in a **rotating** disc of dust and gas called a **nebula**. At the centre of the disc, gravity pulled the gas into a huge, very hot ball – the Sun. Away from the centre of the nebula, smaller balls of gas or rock formed. These were the planets. The Earth is the third planet out from the Sun.

The Earth is about 150 million kilometres (93 million miles) away from the Sun. At this distance, conditions are perfect for life. The Earth is neither too hot nor too cold. It has water and a breathable atmosphere. The atmosphere and the Earth's **magnetic field** protect the surface from the hazards of space.

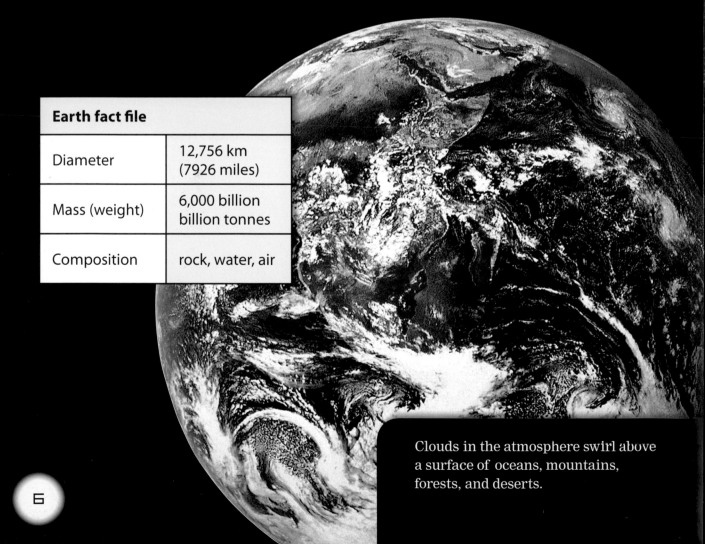

Earth fact file	
Diameter	12,756 km (7926 miles)
Mass (weight)	6,000 billion billion tonnes
Composition	rock, water, air

Clouds in the atmosphere swirl above a surface of oceans, mountains, forests, and deserts.

Looking inside the Earth

We think of the Earth as solid, but much of it is not. It has three layers, called the crust, the mantle, and the core. The core is at the centre. The inside of the core is probably solid and made from pure iron and nickel. The outer part of the core is liquid.

Around the core is the thickest layer – the mantle. The mantle is a mixture of rock and **magma** (**molten** rock). The whole thing is like very thick, lumpy treacle.

On the edge of the Earth

The outermost layer of the Earth is a thin layer called the crust. The crust is solid rock, but it is not all in one piece. The surface is a jigsaw of huge rocky pieces, called plates. It is a bit like a cracked eggshell. A lot of the crust is covered by water. Over two-thirds of the Earth's surface is ocean.

The plates don't stay still, they are continually moving around very, very slowly. Where the plates move together, there are volcanoes and huge mountain ranges. Where they move apart, they create deep trenches. Along the joins there are likely to be earthquakes.

SCIENCE FACT OR SCIENCE FICTION?

In Jules Verne's adventure story *Journey to the Centre of the Earth*, Professor Liedenbrock and his nephew Axel explore a passage in a volcano that leads to the middle of the Earth. At the time the book was written, scientists didn't know whether the centre of the Earth was solid or liquid. We now know that it would be impossible to go down a volcano to the centre of the Earth. The heat from the volcano would kill you before you had even got through the crust.

Protecting the Earth

The whole surface of the Earth is covered by a thin "skin" of gases called the atmosphere. The atmosphere is a layer of air about 100 km (62 miles) thick. It traps some of the Sun's heat near the Earth, which helps to keep us warm. It also protects us from harmful **ultraviolet** light from the Sun. The atmosphere even protects the Earth from being hit by small lumps of rock from space, called **meteoroids**. These burn up in the atmosphere and do not reach the ground.

HOT NEWS:

Not all lumps of rock burn up in the atmosphere. **Meteorites** are large rocks that don't burn up completely. They hit the Earth's surface and can make **craters**. These craters are often difficult to spot, because they have been eroded. Scientists have found at least 170 craters. The largest one found so far is 300 km (185 miles) across and is called Vredefort. It is in South Africa and is about 2 billion years old.

Barringer Meteor Crater in Arizona, USA was created by an iron meteorite crashing into Earth 49,000 years ago. It is 1 km (0.6 mile) across.

The colourful, moving lights of the aurora are best seen near the Arctic and Antarctic circles. However, sometimes you can see them from as far away as London or New York.

Our magnetic field

The Earth has a magnetic field. We use this magnetic field to help us find our way around, by using a magnetic compass, which always points to the north. It is as if there is a giant, solid bar magnet in the centre of the Earth. The Earth's magnetic field is caused by liquid iron moving around in the core of the planet.

Magnetic protection

The Earth's magnetic field is called the **magnetosphere**. It extends thousands of kilometres into space, well beyond the atmosphere. The magnetosphere acts as a second protective shield around the Earth. It sweeps harmful **particles** from the Sun past the Earth, so they can't reach us. However, some tiny particles get through the shield and reach the atmosphere. When they do, they cause the aurora. This is a spectacular display of coloured lights in the sky close to the North and South Poles.

The Moon

The Moon is the Earth's satellite. It is a large ball of rock that orbits the Earth. Earth's gravity keeps the Moon circling only 385,000 km (240,000 miles) away from us. As it orbits, the Moon turns on its **axis**, turning once in every orbit. This means that the same half of the Moon is always facing Earth, so we cannot see the other side.

How big is the Moon?

The Moon is about a quarter of the Earth's **diameter**. It is also less **dense** than the Earth. Together, these two differences mean that gravity on the Moon is weaker. It is about a sixth of the gravity on Earth. The Moon's gravity is not strong enough to keep light gases close to it, so it does not have an atmosphere.

TRY IT YOURSELF:
Watching the wobbles

Although we never see one complete side of the Moon from Earth, over time we can see more than half of it. This is because the Moon wobbles a bit as it orbits. The wobbling is called libration. To see the effects of libration, look at the full Moon and find Mare Crisium. It is a dark patch close to the **equator**, near the edge of the Moon. There is a map on page 44 to help you find it. Draw a circle to represent the Moon, and mark Mare Crisium on it. At the next few full Moons, look for Mare Crisium. Each time mark its position on a circle. Does its distance from the edge change?

A full Moon is a spectacular sight. Using just binoculars, you can examine its surface.

Mare Crisium

Being small makes a difference

Just like the Earth, our Moon has a core, mantle, and crust. But there are important differences. Because it is smaller than the Earth, the inside of the Moon has cooled more quickly. There is no liquid iron in the core, and less molten rock in the mantle.

Because the iron core is not liquid, the Moon does not have a magnetic field. However, scientists can tell from Moon rocks that in the past it did have a strong magnetic field.

No protection

With no atmosphere and no magnetic field, the Moon has no protection from space rocks. The rocks smash into the Moon's surface and create impact craters. Because there is no atmosphere, there is no rain or wind to erode (wear away) the craters. So the Moon's surface is covered in craters. Some have been there for billions of years.

There were six manned Moon landings between 1969 and 1972. The astronauts did many experiments and collected samples of lunar rock.

Making the Moon

For a long time, scientists were not sure how the Moon was made. Until astronauts landed on the Moon in the 1960s and 1970s, there seemed to be three possibilities.

Growing together

One idea was that the Earth and Moon were made at the same time. In space, dust and gas gradually stuck together making little lumps. These lumps crashed into each other and stuck together. They got larger and larger as the gravitational pull between different lumps brought them together. The scientists' idea was that one set of lumps became the Earth, and one became the Moon. If this were true, Moon rocks and Earth rocks would be very similar.

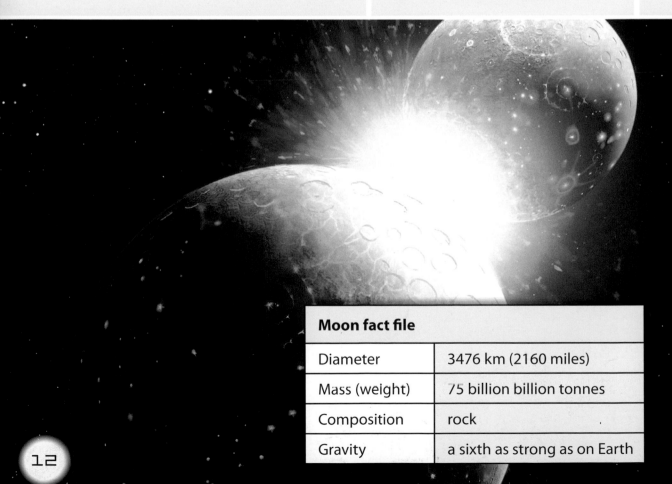

A large planet-like object crashing into Earth is thought to have become the Moon.

Moon fact file	
Diameter	3476 km (2160 miles)
Mass (weight)	75 billion billion tonnes
Composition	rock
Gravity	a sixth as strong as on Earth

Trapping the Moon

Another group of scientists had a different idea. They thought that the Moon came from somewhere a long way away. It travelled through space and then came near to the Earth. The Earth is so large that its gravity trapped the Moon. The Moon then started orbiting around the Earth. If this is how the Moon formed, the rocks on the Moon would be very different to rocks on Earth.

A spinning Earth

The scientists also had good imaginations and wondered what would happen if the Earth spun really fast. They decided that if this had happened, a large chunk of the Earth would have been sent into space and become the Moon. The rocks on the Moon would then be very similar to rocks on Earth. There is some evidence that the Earth used to spin faster, but not that fast!

Moon rocks reveal all

In 1969, Neil Armstrong became the first man to walk on the Moon. He and the other astronauts from the Apollo missions brought Moon rocks back to the Earth. Moon rock is quite similar to Earth rock, but it is not made from exactly the same materials. This suggests that all three of these ideas about how the Moon was made are wrong.

HOT NEWS:
The giant impact theory

Scientists in the mid-1980s finally agreed that a large Solar System object about the size of Mars probably crashed into the Earth 4.5 billion years ago. A mixture of Earth and the mystery body were ejected into space, and these grouped together over time to make the Moon.

Astronauts brought 382 kg (842 lb) of Moon rock, pebbles, sand, and dust back to Earth with them.

Fire and water

There are lots of volcanoes and **lava** (molten rock) flows on Earth, but there are none on the Moon. Looking at the surface of the Moon, scientists have discovered that it did once have lava on or below the surface. They have found dead volcanoes, which are quite small and dome-shaped or cone-shaped. These formed when lava slowly poured through the crust or when lava rose up underneath the surface. Scientists have also found lava plains on the Moon. These are called *maria* ("seas"). The plains formed when very hot, very runny lava flowed out of the ground and spread over a wide area. Most of the plains formed between 3 and 4 billion years ago.

This photograph shows craters and domes that have formed on the Moon's surface.

HOT NEWS:

Finding water

Scientists use spacecraft orbiting the Moon to examine what the Moon is made from. In 1994 the spacecraft *Clementine* examined the surface of the Moon using radio waves. When scientists looked at the results, it seemed that the radio waves were reflecting from something icy. In the late 1990s another spacecraft, *Lunar Prospector*, looked for signs of water on the Moon. The results suggested that there are around 6 billion tonnes of ice on the Moon. This is just about enough water to fill a lake the size of Loch Ness, in Scotland.

Water on the Moon

Some space missions have detected signs of ice on the Moon. Where could this water have come from? Scientists think that it probably came from **comets** or asteroids that crashed into the Moon's surface. If they could examine the Moon's ice, scientists could find out about the comets that have hit the Moon.

Water on the Moon would not survive long in sunlight. It would quickly turn to **water vapour**. The Moon's gravity is not strong enough to keep gas close to the Moon, so the water vapour would disappear into space. If there is water on the Moon, it must be ice. It is most likely to be in the bottom of deep craters that are always in shadow. If there is water hidden in craters, it might be hard for orbiting spacecraft to detect it.

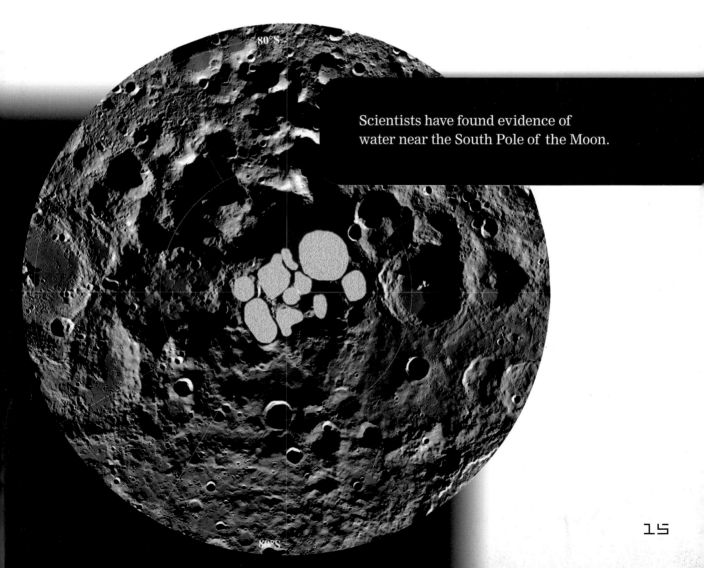

Scientists have found evidence of water near the South Pole of the Moon.

Crash landings

The surface of the Moon is covered with holes. People once thought that these were the craters of volcanoes. Today we know they are impact craters, created when comets, meteoroids, or asteroids crash into the Moon. We have seen that there is no atmosphere on the Moon to slow down or burn up incoming objects. This means that even tiny particles can create craters on the Moon.

Most of the impact craters were created over 3 billion years ago, although there are some younger ones. The largest crater is 2500 km across and 12 km deep.

Tycho is the big, bright crater at the bottom of this picture. It is near the South Pole of the Moon, and easily seen from Earth.

TRY IT YOURSELF:
Find Tycho

Some of the Moon's largest craters are visible from Earth. One younger crater is called Tycho. The crater itself is 85 km (53 miles) across, but its rays cover a quarter of the Moon's circumference. You can see the Tycho Crater from Earth and it is best to observe the rays with your eyes, not a telescope. Look at the south of the Moon. Can you find Tycho Crater?

Tycho Crater

Information from the craters

Scientists can learn about the Moon's craters by looking carefully at them. They can tell when a crater was made and how big the object was that crashed. When something hits the Moon very fast, it can melt the surface. The molten rock fills small craters and is smooth and dark. This makes the cratered regions shinier than the lava "seas" (see page 14).

Around big craters, there are smaller ones created by the bits that got thrown out of the big crater. The younger craters haven't been changed by more recent crashes. They are surrounded by rays – bright streaks of Moon rock reaching out across the surface.

The surface of the Moon is covered in craters, all overlapping each other. Ice could be hidden in the bottom of some of these craters.

The Sun

The Sun is at the centre of the Solar System. It is our nearest star and the star we know most about. However, it is just one of over 200 billion stars in our **galaxy,** the Milky Way. There are billions of other galaxies in the Universe, each containing billions of stars.

The Sun is a huge ball 1,391,020 km (864,340 miles) across, which is 109 times the diameter of Earth. This makes it a medium-sized star.

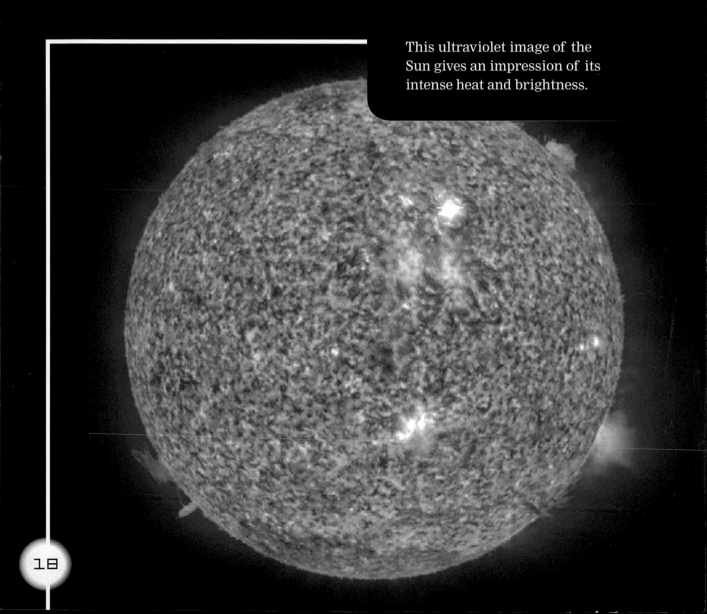

This ultraviolet image of the Sun gives an impression of its intense heat and brightness.

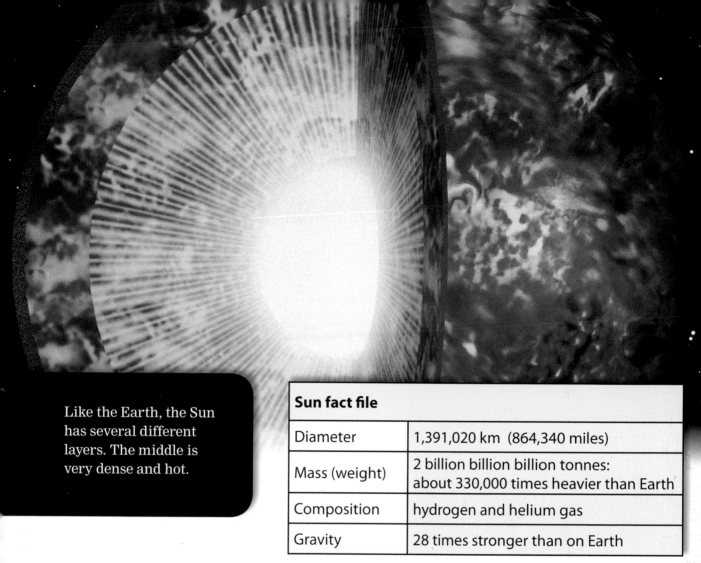

Like the Earth, the Sun has several different layers. The middle is very dense and hot.

Sun fact file	
Diameter	1,391,020 km (864,340 miles)
Mass (weight)	2 billion billion billion tonnes: about 330,000 times heavier than Earth
Composition	hydrogen and helium gas
Gravity	28 times stronger than on Earth

The Sun's layers

The Sun has three layers. In the middle is the core. The core is the hottest part of the Sun. The temperature is an incredible 15.6 million °C (28 million °F) – 10,000 times hotter than a steel furnace. The Sun's core is also very dense. The material in the core is ten times more dense than lead. Heat energy moves out from the core towards the surface.

The middle layer of the Sun is called the radiative zone. In this area, heat **radiation** carries energy very quickly from the centre of the Sun towards the surface.

The outer layer of the Sun is called the **convection** layer. In this layer, energy moves more slowly. Hot bubbles of gas move around, taking heat from the middle of the Sun towards the edge. The temperature of the inner part of the convection zone is about 2 million °C (3.6 million °F). This drops to about 5000 °C (9000 °F) at the surface.

The solar atmosphere

Although the Sun doesn't have a solid surface that we could land on, it does have an atmosphere. The Sun's atmosphere extends above the surface and out into space. Unlike the Earth's atmosphere, it is not one we can breathe.

The layers of the atmosphere

We can only see light from one layer of the Sun. This is called the photosphere. The photosphere is the innermost layer of the Sun's atmosphere. It is the layer that emits the light that we see. It is a thin layer, only about 480 km (300 miles) thick.

Covering the photosphere is the chromosphere. This is about 2500 km (1550 miles) thick. Beyond this is the corona, the Sun's outermost layer. It is several times thicker than the Sun's diameter. Although the corona emits light, it is so faint that we can only see it from Earth during a total **eclipse**. However, scientists can study the corona using special telescopes (see pages 38–39).

The Sun's photosphere is not smooth. It seems to look very grainy and be covered in little pockets of material.

WARNING!

Never look directly at the Sun! The Sun emits so much light that it is very dangerous to look at it directly. It will burn your eyes and damage them for ever. It could even make you go blind. Even sunglasses cannot protect your eyes. To look at the Sun, scientists use special telescopes with very strong filters.

Hotter, not colder

The temperature of the Sun's surface is 4500–6000 °C (8100–10,800 °F) but the corona can reach 2 million °C (3.6 million °F). When you move away from something that is hot, you should get cooler. For some reason the Sun doesn't work like this and scientists are not yet sure why this is.

HOW IT WORKS:
Filtered light

Visible light is not the only kind of energy coming from the Sun. Light is only one kind of radiation. There are many other kinds, ranging from low-energy radio waves, through infra-red, visible light, and ultraviolet to high-energy X-rays. To study the Sun's layers, scientists use telescopes that can see different kinds of radiation. They use filters to cut out all radiation except one type. For instance, a filter that shows only certain X-rays gives a picture of the corona – the outermost layer of the Sun's atmosphere.

The Sun extends out into space, as arcs and loops of material rise above the surface.

Energy from the Sun

The centre of the Sun is like a huge nuclear reactor. It burns nearly 700 million tonnes of hydrogen gas every second. Five million tonnes turns into energy and the rest turns into a heavier gas called helium. It may seem as if the Sun is burning a lot of hydrogen very quickly, but it has burned only a tiny fraction of its mass in 4.5 billion years.

Light and heat energy

Enormous amounts of light and heat energy pour out of the Sun and into space. This light and heat spreads through the Solar System. The further away from the Sun you are, the less light and heat you can get. On Earth, we are lucky to have enough light and heat to grow crops to feed us and provide us with fuel. On Pluto, which is much further from the Sun, there is not enough light or warmth to grow anything.

Energy from the Sun is used by plants, like these crops, to help them grow. We then harvest them and turn them into food.

HOW IT WORKS:
The ozone hole

Over the Antarctic there is an area where there is hardly any ozone in the upper atmosphere and more ultraviolet light reaches the Earth's surface. This "ozone hole" can get quite big, especially in summer, making it dangerous to be outside without covering up. The ozone layer over the Arctic also gets thinner in the summer. Scientists have found that a group of chemicals called CFCs damage the ozone layer, and have created the ozone hole. CFCs are used in aerosol sprays and in fridges. Less damaging chemicals are now being used instead of CFCs wherever possible.

Dangerous light

Not all the energy from the Sun is useful. The Sun also sends out ultraviolet light, which can burn our skin and cause skin cancer. However, the Earth's atmosphere protects us from most ultraviolet light. In the upper part of the atmosphere there is a layer that contains large amounts of the gas **ozone**. Ozone absorbs ultraviolet light very well. Without it, life would be very different.

In space, astronauts have to be careful because there is no atmosphere to protect them from the harmful ultraviolet light. If they were in space for a long time, maybe on their way to Mars, they would also have to avoid other dangerous types of radiation from the Sun.

The magnetic Sun

The Sun, the Earth, and some of the other planets behave as if they have giant magnets inside them. A magnet affects the space around it. It has a force that pulls at some metals, such as iron, but doesn't pull at other metals, such as aluminium. The further you are from the magnet, the weaker the pull of the magnet. If you move a small compass around the magnet, the needle will keep changing direction. If you have a bar magnet, you can dust iron filings around it. The iron filings are attracted to the magnet, but are not pulled very far. They link up in lines to show the shape of the magnetic field. It curves around from the North Pole of the magnet to the South Pole.

The Sun's magnetic field

Like the Earth, the Sun has a magnetic field that stretches far out into space. When the Sun is "quiet" the magnetic field looks like the magnetic field surrounding a bar magnet, and is quite simple. However, the Sun's magnetic field doesn't stay like this.

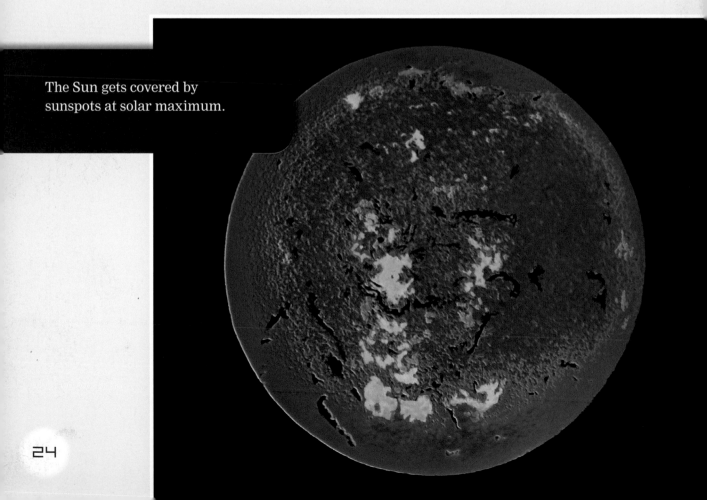

The Sun gets covered by sunspots at solar maximum.

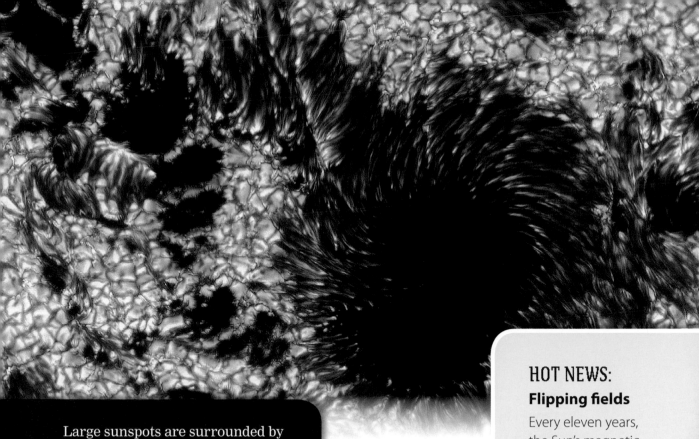

Large sunspots are surrounded by smaller ones. The sunspots churn up the surface of the Sun.

Sunspots

The Sun frequently gets spotty. These spots show where the magnetic field on the Sun is very strong. The spots come in pairs. From one spot, the magnetic field points "north" and from the other it points "south". During this time, the Sun's magnetic field looks less and less like that of a bar magnet. There are bits popping up and down all over the place.

The number of **sunspots** and the shape of the Sun's magnetic field varies in an eleven-year cycle. There are more spots near the **poles** at the start of the cycle (solar minimum). Near the middle of the cycle there are more spots at the equator (solar maximum). The number of sunspots then decreases again until the next cycle starts. There are more sunspots in total at solar maximum than there are at solar minimum.

HOT NEWS:
Flipping fields

Every eleven years, the Sun's magnetic field flips. The north and south magnetic poles swap round at solar maximum. In the past the Earth's magnetic field has flipped over too. On average, the Earth's magnetic field flips 4 or 5 times every million years. The last reversal was about 800,000 years ago, and some scientists are predicting another flip in 1500 years time.

The active Sun

The Sun never stays the same. Things are changing all the time. Using special telescopes equipped to look at the different kinds of radiation coming from the Sun, scientists have been able watch how the Sun changes over minutes, days, and months. They have made some amazing discoveries.

Going round

Like the Earth, the Sun rotates. However, because it is made of gas rather than being solid, it does not all rotate at the same time! The area round the equator moves fastest. This goes round once every 25 days or so. In the areas away from the equator and towards the poles, the rotation is slower. The polar regions go round once every 35 days.

Some solar flares are so powerful that they can disrupt satellite systems and telecommunications on Earth.

BIOGRAPHY:

Galileo Galilei (1564–1642)

Galileo was born in Pisa, Italy. His father was a musician, but Galileo became a scientist. He is often called the "father of science" because he laid the foundations for scientific study in many subjects. In 1609 Galileo designed and built one of the first telescopes. He used it to look at the Sun just as it set. He discovered sunspots, and saw that they moved across the disc of the Sun. From this he worked out that the Sun was rotating. Sadly, these Sun studies damaged Galileo's eyes, and in later life he went blind.

Giant loops of hot material called coronal loops extend thousands of kilometres above the surface of the Sun. They can be much bigger than the Earth.

Solar explosions

All kinds of storms and explosions happen in the Sun's atmosphere. One kind of "storm" is called a solar flare. Because different parts of the Sun go round at different rates, the Sun's magnetic field gets wound up, like an elastic band. Scientists think that solar flares happen when the energy stored in the magnetic field is released. When this happens, scientists see bursts of X-rays and ultraviolet light.

A coronal mass ejection is the largest type of eruption that comes from the Sun. A mass ejection can send billions of tonnes of material out into the Solar System. Sometimes this material heads towards the Earth. The material affects the Earth's magnetosphere (magnetic field), causing it to change shape. Some of the particles enter the magnetosphere and cause the aurora (see page 9). After a coronal mass ejection, you might be able to see the aurora when you are quite far from the North and South Poles. The particles can also cause damage to communications and electrical systems on Earth.

Coronal loops are arches of incredibly hot gas that can extend thousands of kilometres into the Sun's corona.

Earth and Sun

The Earth, Sun, and Moon move around each other in space. The Earth and the other planets orbit around the Sun, and the Moon orbits around the Earth. At the same time, the Sun, Earth, and Moon are all rotating.

Rotating in space

Imagine a line stretching through the middle of the Earth, from the North Pole to the South Pole. This is the rotational axis of the Earth. The Earth rotates around this axis once every 24 hours. As the Earth rotates, different parts of it face the Sun. It is daytime where the Earth is in sunlight and night-time where the Earth is in the Sun's shadow.

If the Earth's axis was parallel to the Sun's axis of rotation, day and night would be equal lengths all over the world. However, the Earth's axis is tilted slightly. Because of this, the number of hours of daylight and darkness vary, depending on the time of year and where you are on the Earth.

Moving across the sky

As the Earth rotates, the Sun appears to move in an arc above the horizon. It rises in the east and sets in the west. It is at its highest point at midday. During the day, shadows on Earth change length. Shadows are shortest at midday, when the Sun is highest. They are longest at sunrise and sunset.

During the day, the Sun moves across the sky in a curve. It reaches the highest point at midday.

The length of the day

Near the equator, days and nights are close to the same length, about 12 hours long. Away from the equator, the length of day and night depends on the season. As the Earth's axis is tilted, the days are longer and the nights are shorter in the summer. If you live near the North or South Poles, the Sun never sets in the summer. In the winter, the nights are longer and near the poles, it hardly gets light at all.

TRY IT YOURSELF:

Find out when the Sun rises and sets this week. Look in a paper or on the Internet. Sunrise and sunset times will depend on where you live and what time of year it is. Can you find out how long your longest day is?

As the Sun sets, the sky turns fiery reds and oranges. This happens because particles in the atmosphere scatter the light from the Sun.

Seasons

What time of year is it? If it's nice and warm, it might be summer or spring. If the weather is cooler and wetter, it might be autumn or winter. The Earth rotates on its axis, but it also **revolves** around the Sun. If you looked down on the Earth and Sun from above, while you were hovering over the North Pole of the Sun, you wouldn't actually see the North Pole of the Earth. This is because the Earth is tilted over slightly. This tilt is very important – it is the reason we have seasons.

Changing amounts of light

The tilt of the Earth's axis means that some parts of the Earth have more hours of daylight than others. When the North Pole is tilted towards the Sun, the South Pole is tilted away from the Sun. Then, the northern **hemisphere** gets more light and the southern hemisphere gets less light. Later in the year, the Earth has moved so that the North Pole is tilted away from the Sun and the South Pole is tilted towards the Sun. Then, the northern hemisphere gets less light and the southern hemisphere gets more.

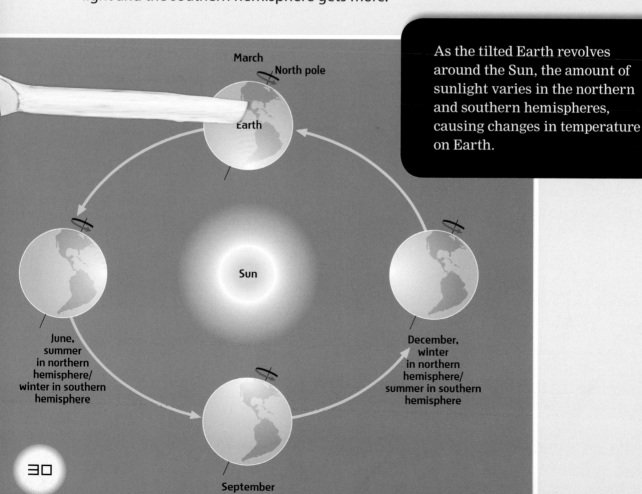

As the tilted Earth revolves around the Sun, the amount of sunlight varies in the northern and southern hemispheres, causing changes in temperature on Earth.

March

North pole

Earth

Sun

June,
summer
in northern
hemisphere/
winter in southern
hemisphere

December,
winter
in northern
hemisphere/
summer in southern
hemisphere

September

Spring, summer, autumn, and winter

With more light, the land and sea can heat up as they store heat energy from the Sun. Whichever hemisphere you are in, when there are the most hours of daylight, it is summer. When there are fewer hours of daylight, it is winter. In between winter and summer is spring, and between summer and winter is autumn.

Differences between north and south

When it is summer in the northern hemisphere, it is winter in the southern hemisphere. Similarly, when it is winter in the northern hemisphere, it is summer in the southern hemisphere. Autumn and spring swap around too. Near the equator, the amount of daylight doesn't change much during the year. However, the North and South Poles have 24 hours of daylight in summer and 24 hours of night-time in winter.

BIOGRAPHY:

Egnatio Pellegrino Rainaldi Danti (1536–1586)

Egnatio was a key figure in the history of today's calendar. Like his father, Danti made astronomical instruments and was a clever mathematician. In 1574, he observed that on March 11 the night and day were the same length. This should happen on the **equinox**, March 22. Danti realized that the calendar did not match the actual movement of the Earth around the Sun. His discovery contributed to a change in the calendar. Pope Gregory XIII (left) changed the calendar in the 1580s so that leap days were only added in centuries that could be divided by 400. The Gregorian calendar was adopted in Great Britain in 1752.

Years

A year is the length of time that it takes a planet to travel once round the Sun and get back to the place it started. It takes 365.24 days for the Earth to orbit the Sun, so this is the length of an Earth year.

Our calendar year is 365 days, which is about 6 hours shorter than the actual time it takes the Earth to go round the Sun. So, every year we are about a quarter of a day behind where we should be. If the calendar stayed like this, after about 730 years summer in the northern hemisphere would be in December and summer in the southern hemisphere would be in June!

It is midnight in summer near the North Pole, and the Sun still hasn't set! In winter, it would be nearly dark at midday.

Stonehenge may have been built as an astronomical clock. On the summer solstice (the longest day of the year) the Sun shines between some of the stones.

Leap years

To make life less confusing, every four years there is an extra day added to the calendar year. This day is called a leap day, and the year when it is added is called a leap year. Leap years take place if you can divide the year by four, so 2008 and 2012 will be leap years.

As an Earth year is just over 365 days, other small corrections have to be made to the calendar to keep it in step with the seasons. Centuries are not leap years unless you can divide the year by 400. The year 2000 was a leap year, but 2100 and 2200 will not be.

Earth and Moon

The Moon is the brightest object we can see in the night sky. Yet the Moon is not a fiery ball of gas like the Sun. We can only see it when light from the Sun reflects off the Moon's surface.

Months

Just as the Earth revolves around the Sun, the Moon revolves around the Earth. It takes the Moon 27.3 days to orbit the Earth, but because the Earth is orbiting the Sun, it takes a bit longer (29.5 days) for the Moon to return to the same place with respect to the Sun. We call this the **lunar cycle**.

The months of the year were at one time linked to the time it takes the Moon to orbit the Earth. The twelve months of the modern calendar do not link up with the cycles of the Moon. However in other calendars, such as the Chinese traditional calendar and the Islamic religious calendar, the months do link up with the lunar cycle.

When the Moon is low in the sky, it seems to be bigger. Your eyes are tricked because it is closer to things you know the size of.

TRY IT YOURSELF:

Over a month, keep a record of the Moon. Draw 31 circles and mark on one day the amount of the Moon you can see. How long does it take to go from full Moon to full Moon?

New Moons

If you look at the Moon every day over a month, it doesn't always look the same. This is because we can only see the parts of the Moon that are lit by the Sun. At the start of the lunar cycle, the Moon is between the Sun and the Earth. There is no sunlight reaching the side of the Moon facing Earth, so you can only see the smallest sliver of the Moon. This is called a new Moon. The new Moon rises around sunrise and sets around sunset.

The quarter Moon

On the nights after the new Moon you begin to see the sunlit side of the Moon. After about seven days you can see one quarter of the entire Moon. The other quarter of the Moon that is facing you is in shadow, so you can't see it. The quarter Moon rises at about midday and sets about midnight.

The full Moon

Just over seven days later, the Moon is on the opposite side of the Earth from the Sun, and you can see the full disk. This is called a full Moon.

There are eight phases of the Moon:

1. new Moon
2. waxing crescent Moon
3. first quarter Moon
4. waxing gibbous Moon
5. full Moon
6. waning gibbous Moon
7. last quarter Moon
8. waning crescent Moon.

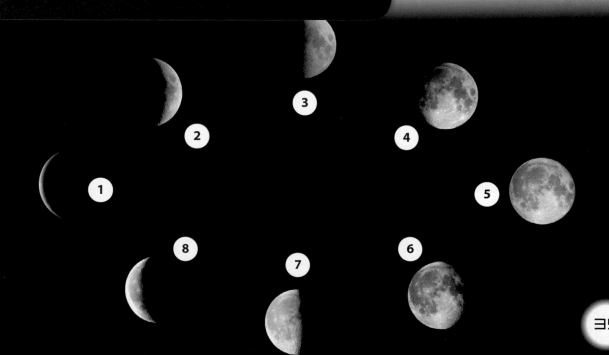

Tides

Although the Moon's gravity is not as strong as the Earth's and it is far away from the Earth, the Moon's gravity still affects us. The Moon is continually pulling the oceans and the Earth towards it. This is called a tidal bulge.

High and low tides

Imagine you are standing by the sea on the side of the Earth closest to the Moon. As it is closest to the Moon, this side of the Earth experiences the strongest gravitational pull from the Moon. The oceans are pulled most strongly and form a bulge, which causes a high tide. As the Earth is turning all the time, the tidal bulge is actually just ahead of the imaginary line between the Earth and the Moon.

Just over 6 hours later, the Earth has made a quarter turn. You are now further away from the Moon, so the effect of gravity is weaker and the Moon doesn't pull the water here towards it so strongly. In the sea, the water level drops and you see a low tide.

During the day, the sea rises and falls. You can see more of the beach at low tide.

Furthest away from the Moon

Wait for another 6 hours or so and you are now on the side of the Earth furthest from the Moon. As the Moon's gravity is weakest here, you might expect a low tide. However, this doesn't happen. The Moon still pulls the Earth and the oceans but the Earth is pulled more towards the Moon than the oceans. There is a bulge of water on this side, making another high tide. If you wait just over 6 hours again, you will see another low tide.

HOT NEWS:
Longer days

The tidal bulge of water moves around the Earth. Moving anything needs energy and moving giant bulges of water needs a lot of energy. Very gradually, the Earth loses energy as a result of moving the tides. As it loses energy it rotates more slowly. This means that in the past, days on Earth were shorter than they are now!

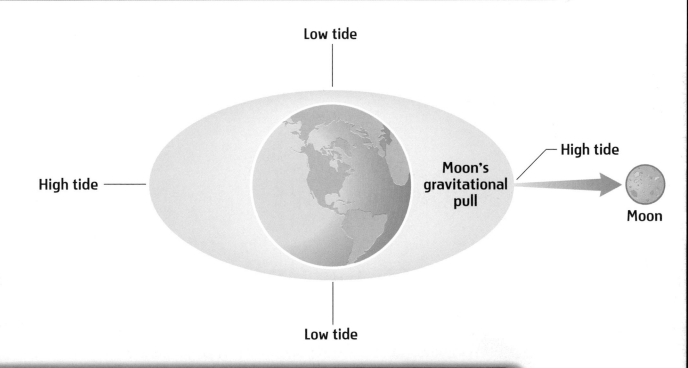

Low tide

High tide

Moon's gravitational pull

High tide

Moon

Low tide

There are two high tides and two low tides every day. These happen because the Moon's gravity tugs at the oceans and the Earth. As the Earth rotates, the water in the oceans rises and falls.

Solar eclipses

Solar eclipses are when the Moon casts a shadow on the Earth. They occur when the Moon is directly between the Earth and the Sun. The Moon casts a shadow on Earth, blocking out some or all the sunlight. Eclipses on Earth are special because the diameter of the Sun is about 400 times the Moon's diameter. The Sun is also 400 times further away from the Earth than the Moon. So from Earth, the Moon appears to be about the same size as the Sun.

The Moon changes size

The Moon's orbit is an **ellipse**, not a circle, so the distance between the Earth and the Moon varies during each orbit – by about 50,000 km (31,000 miles). Because of this, the Moon seems to change size in the sky slightly as it orbits the Earth.

HOW IT WORKS:

As the Moon orbits the Earth every month, it must keep coming in between the Earth and the Sun, so why don't we have an eclipse every month? This is because the Earth, Sun, and Moon don't always travel in space on the same plane. If you could draw a line between the Earth and the Sun, you would see that the Moon is normally above or below the line.

During a total eclipse, the Moon completely covers the Sun, and suddenly you can see the hot gases streaming out into space.

Different kinds of eclipse

During an eclipse, if the Moon is at the point in its orbit when it is closer to the Earth, it completely covers the Sun. This is called a total solar eclipse. However, if the eclipse happens when the Moon is further away from the Earth, the Moon appears smaller in the sky and does not totally cover the Sun. On Earth, you see a ring of light called an annular eclipse.

During an eclipse, the Moon's shadow only covers a small part of the Earth's surface. You can only see an eclipse if you are in this area. Around the edges of the shadow, you will see a partial eclipse. Here, the Moon appears to bite into the edge of the Sun, but it doesn't cover it completely.

TRY IT YOURSELF:

You may be lucky enough to live where there is going to be a solar eclipse. You must never look directly at the Sun during an eclipse, even with sunglasses or with a telescope. The Sun is very powerful and will permanently damage your eyes. You can use safe solar filters to look at the Sun.

Lunar eclipses

Just like solar eclipses, lunar eclipses happen when something is in shadow. For lunar eclipses it is the Moon that is in shadow of the Earth. When the Earth moves between the Sun and the Moon, the Earth casts a shadow on the Moon.

The red Moon

If the Moon was completely in shadow, we would not be able to see it at all during a lunar eclipse. However, a small amount of light from the Sun does reach the Moon. This light is refracted (bent) around the edges of the Earth by the atmosphere.

During a lunar eclipse, the Moon can appear quite red. This is because other colours in the sunlight are absorbed by the atmosphere. As a result, the light that falls on the Moon is red.

During a lunar eclipse, the Moon turns a reddish-brown colour. You can still see some of the craters.

TRY IT YOURSELF:
How big is the Moon?

On a night when there is a full Moon, look at the Moon when it is rising. How big does it look? Now look at the Moon when it is higher in the sky. Does it look bigger or smaller? Does it make any difference if you turn your head upside down and look at the Moon? Hold different-sized coins at arm's length. What size coin do you need to cover the Moon? Does it make any difference whether the Moon has just risen or is higher in the sky?

During a lunar eclipse, the Earth casts a shadow on the Moon.

Types of eclipse

There are three types of lunar eclipse: partial, total (these are both easy to see), and penumbral (these are hard to see).

• Partial eclipses – part of the full Moon passes through the Earth's shadow.

• Total eclipses – the whole of the full Moon passes through the Earth's shadow.

• Penumbral eclipses – the Earth blocks out some the Sun's light but not all of it.

How often do they happen?

Lunar eclipses happen when there would normally be a full Moon. As we discovered with solar eclipses, if the Moon orbited the Earth in the same plane as the Earth orbits the Sun, there would be an eclipse every month. However, the Moon is normally above or below the Earth's shadow. Total lunar eclipses happen somewhere on Earth about once every six months.

The death of the Sun

The Sun is not going to last forever. It is in the middle of its life, but still has fuel for about another 4 billion years. One day, all the hydrogen in its core will be used up. All that will be left in the middle is helium. When this happens, the pull of gravity will cause the core of the Sun to collapse.

A cool giant

The outer layers of the Sun will not collapse like the core. They will expand and become cooler (although they will still be very hot). The Sun will become so big that the planet Mercury will be inside it.

Although the Sun itself will be cooler, it will have grown a lot, so the Earth will be closer to its surface. This means that the Earth will get much hotter. The atmosphere will disappear, the surface will melt, and there will be no life on the planet.

Eventually the outer layers of the Sun will expand and drift away. They will form something called a planetary nebula.

This is a photograph of the red giant Betelgeuse. Scientists think that the Sun will eventually expand to become a red giant too.

The Sun shrinks

As the core of the Sun gets smaller and smaller, the temperature in the middle will get hotter. At some point, it will be hot enough to burn the helium. When the helium burns it will turn into carbon. When all the helium has been burnt, the core of the Sun will shrink again. By this time it will be incredibly dense. One cup of material from the core will weigh about 50 tonnes! The Sun will become a **white dwarf** star.

Eventually, the white dwarf will cool into a black dwarf. The Universe has not existed long enough for any white dwarfs to have cooled down this much. As far as we know, no black dwarfs exist. Our Sun will become the first.

HOW IT WORKS:

Stars more than eight times bigger than the Sun end in a more dramatic way. When all their fuel runs out there is an incredibly big explosion called a supernova. The core of the star usually collapses to a very small black lump called a neutron star. But if the star is really big, the core carries on collapsing until it becomes a **black hole**.

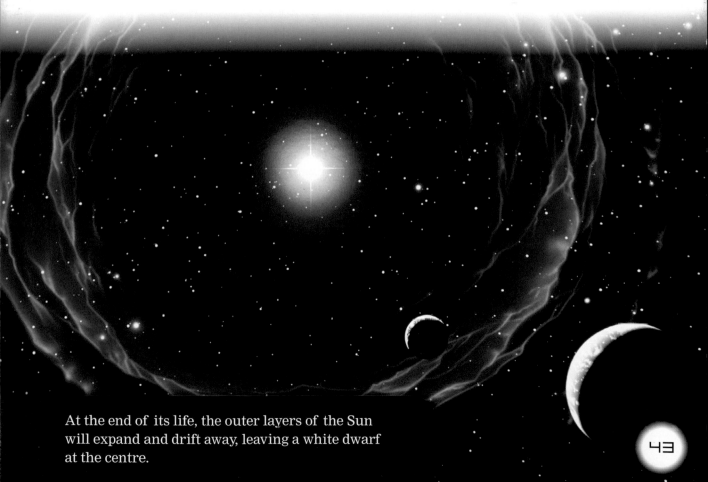

At the end of its life, the outer layers of the Sun will expand and drift away, leaving a white dwarf at the centre.

Map of the Moon

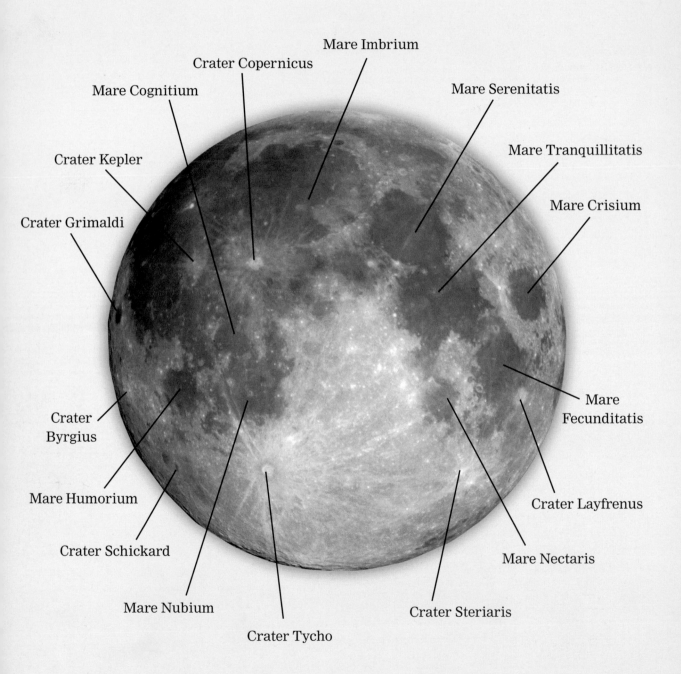

Mare Imbrium

Crater Copernicus

Mare Cognitium

Mare Serenitatis

Mare Tranquillitatis

Crater Kepler

Mare Crisium

Crater Grimaldi

Crater Byrgius

Mare Fecunditatis

Mare Humorium

Crater Layfrenus

Crater Schickard

Mare Nubium

Crater Steriaris

Mare Nectaris

Crater Tycho

Eclipse timetable

Solar eclipses

These are the dates for solar eclipses until 2010:

22 Sep 2006	Annular	South America, west Africa, Antarctica
19 Mar 2007	Partial	Asia, Alaska
11 Sep 2007	Partial	South America, Antarctica
07 Feb 2008	Annular	Antarctica, eastern Australia, New Zealand
01 Aug 2008	Total	north-east N. America, Europe, Asia
26 Jan 2009	Annular	southern Africa, Antarctica, South-East Asia, Australia
22 Jul 2009	Total	eastern Asia, Pacific Ocean, Hawaii
15 Jan 2010	Annular	Africa, Asia
11 Jul 2010	Total	southern S. America

When can I see them?

These are the dates of partial and total lunar eclipses until 2010:

07 Sep 2006	Partial	Europe, Africa, Asia, Australia
03 Mar 2007	Total	Americas, Europe, Africa, Asia
28 Aug 2007	Total	eastern Asia, Australia, Pacific, Americas
21 Feb 2008	Total	central Pacific, Americas, Europe, Africa
16 Aug 2008	Partial	South America, Europe, Africa, Asia, Australia
31 Dec 2009	Partial	Europe, Africa, Asia, Australia
26 Jun 2010	Partial	eastern Asia, Australia, Pacific, western America
21 Dec 2010	Total	eastern Asia, Australia, Pacific, Americas, Europe

Glossary

asteroid minor planet orbiting the Sun

atmosphere gas held by gravity around a planet or moon

axis an imaginary line around which something rotates

black hole tiny, dead star so dense that even light cannot escape

comet a large block of ice, rock, and dust that orbits the Sun

convection movement of hot material upwards and cooler material downwards

crater hole or depression on the surface of an astronomical body caused by the impact of a comet or meteorite

dense heavy for its size

diameter the width of a circle or a sphere (ball)

eclipse when one astronomical object blocks the light from another

ellipse oval shape

equator imaginary line around the middle of a planet, moon or the Sun

equinox the two days during the year when day and night are the same length

force push or a pull

galaxy huge "island" of billions of stars in space

gravity force that pulls objects together

hemisphere one half of a sphere

lava molten rock on the Earth's surface

lunar cycle time between full Moons

magma molten rock

magnetic field lines of force around a magnetic object

magnetosphere region of the Earth's magnetic sphere

mass the quantity of matter in an object

meteorite space rock that hits the surface of another planet

meteoroids small fragments of rock or metal that may be pieces of planets, moons, comets or asteroids

molten melted, turned into liquid by heat

moon rocky body orbiting a planet

nebula cloud of gas and dust in space

orbit the path of an astronomical object moving around another

ozone form of oxygen gas that is found in a layer in the Earth's upper atmosphere

particle a small piece of something

planet large body of rock or gas that orbits the Sun or another star

pole one of the two points on a planet or moon, furthest from the equator

radiation energy carried by rays or waves such as light rays

revolve to turn around

rotate to turn around on an axis

Solar System the planets and their moons, asteroids, comets, meteoroids, etc. that orbit the Sun

sunspot dark region on the Sun

ultraviolet type of high–energy light

water vapour water in the form of a gas

white dwarf small, dense star near the end of its life

Further information

Books

Encyclopedia of Space, Heather Couper and Nigel Henbest (Dorling Kindersley, 2003)

How to Get to the Moon, Hazel Richardson (Oxford University Press,1999)

The Night Sky, Nigel Henbest (Usborne, 2000)

Space Odyssey: Voyage to the Planets Mission Report, Steve Cole (Dorling Kindersley, 2004)

Telescopes and Observatories, Heather Couper and Nigel Henbest (Franklin Watts, 1987)

Places to visit

Royal Observatory
Greenwich
London
SE10 9NF
UK
+44 (0)20 8312 6565
www.rog.nmm.ac.uk/

Siding Spring Observatory
Coonabarabran
National Park Road
New South Wales
Australia
+64 (0)2 68-426211
www.sidingspringexploratory.com.au

Websites

Windows to the Universe: history and people
http://www.windows.ucar.edu/tour/link=/people/people.html
A user-friendly guide to the Earth and space science. There are easy, intermediate, and advanced versions of each article, so you can choose the level you want to read at.

Space and beyond *http://kids.msfc.nasa.gov/Space/*
A website about stars, black holes, quasars, and other space stuff, from NASA. Also includes Astronomy Picture of the Day.

Hubble gallery *http://hubblesite.org/gallery/*
A gallery of pictures and movies from the Hubble Space Telescope.

Index

Titles in the *Stargazers' Guides* series include:

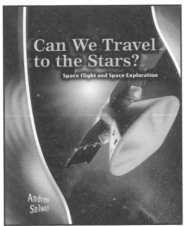

Hardback   0 431 18190 X

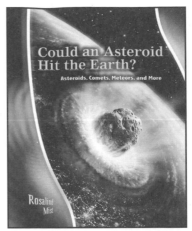

Hardback   0 431 18188 8

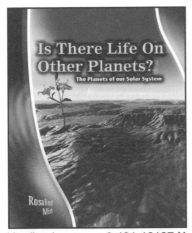

Hardback   0 431 18187 X

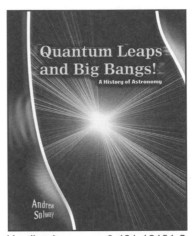

Hardback   0 431 18191 8

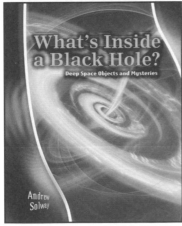

Hardback   0 431 18189 6

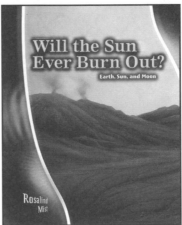

Hardback   0 431 18186 1

Find out about other titles from Heinemann Library on our website www.heinemann.co.uk/library